Bob 'Idea Man' Hooey
Author of Legacy of Leadership

# POCKET WISDOM
## *for* **LEADERS**

## THE POWER OF ONE!

Leadership is a contact sport – you lead when you have
positive contact and inspiration with your teams.

1

# Welcome...

My purpose in creating **The Power of ONE!** motivational book is to provide you with a *positive dose* of inspiration or leadership sampler and *food for thought*.

> **"What you leave behind is not what is engraved in stone monuments; but is woven into the lives of others."** Pericles

**An inspirational thought** to help you focus your mind on the positive while looking for new opportunities to grow; to hone your skills; to gain expertise; and to be better equipped to serve, coach, and lead your teams to greater success.

**A provocative thought** to remind you to leverage your efforts in building long-term, mutually beneficial relationships which generate amazing personal and professional growth. Successful results based on your *continued* investment in honing your skills.

When you dare to follow your beliefs and take ***personal responsibility*** for your own life – you impact everyone around you. That positive, personal leadership choice has a ***ripple effect*** that changes the world. Entire industries have been sparked by one person who dared to take on personal leadership. That is why the greatest people throughout time are *still* remembered in history books and in the lives of those they led and impacted.

You can profitably take your career, company, or community to the next level. **The world needs more leadership, will you step up and claim yours?**

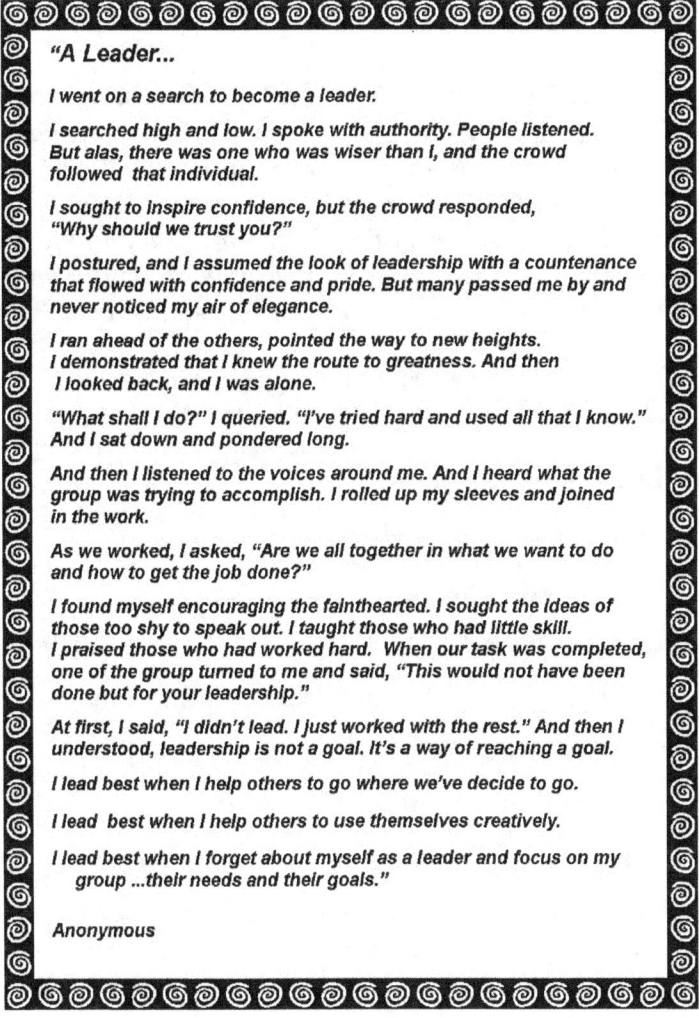

**"A Leader...**

I went on a search to become a leader.

I searched high and low. I spoke with authority. People listened. But alas, there was one who was wiser than I, and the crowd followed that individual.

I sought to inspire confidence, but the crowd responded, "Why should we trust you?"

I postured, and I assumed the look of leadership with a countenance that flowed with confidence and pride. But many passed me by and never noticed my air of elegance.

I ran ahead of the others, pointed the way to new heights. I demonstrated that I knew the route to greatness. And then I looked back, and I was alone.

"What shall I do?" I queried. "I've tried hard and used all that I know." And I sat down and pondered long.

And then I listened to the voices around me. And I heard what the group was trying to accomplish. I rolled up my sleeves and joined in the work.

As we worked, I asked, "Are we all together in what we want to do and how to get the job done?"

I found myself encouraging the fainthearted. I sought the ideas of those too shy to speak out. I taught those who had little skill. I praised those who had worked hard. When our task was completed, one of the group turned to me and said, "This would not have been done but for your leadership."

At first, I said, "I didn't lead. I just worked with the rest." And then I understood, leadership is not a goal. It's a way of reaching a goal.

I lead best when I help others to go where we've decide to go.

I lead best when I help others to use themselves creatively.

I lead best when I forget about myself as a leader and focus on my group ...their needs and their goals."

Anonymous

*"When you unleash 'The Power of ONE!' you inflame the passion of many... and you truly walk 'In the Company of Leaders'." Bob 'Idea Man' Hooey*
www.ideaman.net

3

# Leadership observations

*"Learning is the essential fuel for leaders, the source of high-octane energy that keeps up the momentum by continually sparking new understanding, new ideas, and new challenges. It is indispensable under today's conditions of rapid change and complexity. Very simply, those who do not learn do not long survive as leaders."* **Warren Bevis & Burt Nanus**

Let me share some leadership ideas drawn from my observations of a wide range of leaders over the years.

**Leaders are not born**

**Leaders are open to change**

**Leaders are creative**

**Leaders make mistakes and build on lessons learned**

**Leaders are forged in the heat of reality, moulded on the anvil of adversity, by the hammers of life**

**Leaders are more often avid readers**

**Leaders are the foundation of success for their teams**

Give some thought to these foundational leadership ideas and see how they apply to your journey. The world needs more effective leaders and you have it within you to be one of them.

*"The primary role of the strong, effective leader is to recruit, engage, and empower other strong leaders."*
**Bob 'Idea Man' Hooey**

# Getting started

Welcome to the *never-ending* journey of an evolving career and management focus on personal leadership development and coaching. Changes in global perspective has placed a new focus and pressure on finding and applying more productive uses of our assets and updating our employees' skills to compete successfully.

Taking **personal leadership** in your own career growth and success is worth the investment. This is where you apply strategic *'leverage'* to dynamically succeed!

Too many leaders are blind to the opportunities and responsibilities of creating and nurturing those who would follow them. Too many miss the opportunity (are blind) to play an active part in the selection and growth of those who would succeed them.

> *"Avoid being the blind leading the blind…*
> *leave behind A Legacy of Leadership."*
> **Bob 'Idea Man' Hooey**

There is an increased acceptance of using personal leadership and coaching in the workplace. In the past, coaching has been regulated or known only as a remedial method of helping employees improve *'sagging'* or deficient performance. It still has a valid use in this area.

Recently, workplace coaching has found a new focus. Leading edge employees, managers, and executives have been experiencing positive results from enlisting the help of a leadership coach to help them improve in specific areas or to achieve specific goals.

**People have been going 'outside' the corporate arena and enlisting or recruiting personal or leadership coaches. They want to change, to improve their performance, and to enhance their ability to win!**

Many world leaders, executives, and managers have also seen the wisdom and a positive return on their investment of time and resources in training and **coaching their employees and future leaders for *'optimal'* results**.

Things are changing in the boardrooms and on the sales floors of businesses across North America and around the globe as competition heats up for world markets.

**People experience problems and challenges in their performance for four major reasons:**

- Poor or inadequate training
- Inadequate equipment or support services
- Time constraints and poor time management
- Motivation

Unfortunately, many of these reasons can be traced back to poor or uninspired leadership.

Many 21$^{st}$ century leaders are moving into the coaching role as an effective style and skill in helping their teams grow and succeed.

**Leadership coaching** in its essence will help you discover the area(s) which are acting as roadblocks for the person being coached.

**Leadership coaching** can help you turn roadblocks into stepping-stones for increased success, productivity, and a real sense of satisfaction on the job.

**Leadership coaching** can bring you a sense of satisfaction as the coach, too – **in bringing out the best and in seeing your people win!**

One of the most important aspects of your leadership growth and continued success is measured by the investment in your team and the noticeable and proven results of those efforts.

> *"You win when your people win!"*
> **Bob 'Idea Man' Hooey**

**I had the opportunity to repeatedly drive this idea home a few years back when I was brought in to work with the President and senior management team for one of Canada's 50 Best Managed (retail) Companies.**

Over a period of four months, we explored ways of helping them hone their leadership skills to better lead their respective teams. We also worked on strategies to powerfully expand their reach. The results were astounding! The following year they broke the billion-dollar retail sales mark for the first time in their 33-year history.

This is a lesson learned from working with and studying the actions of North America's leaders in various industries, including the volunteer sector. This, coupled with my own experience in a variety of leadership roles, has reinforced my contention that *"You win when your team wins!"*

# Bob's Seven Laws of Leadership

The following areas are for your consideration. From years of observation and experience, I feel you need these skills/qualities to be effective and influential in your leadership.

**Example** – are you dependable?

**Communication** – is it clear, concise?

**Ability** – are you capable to lead?

**Motivation** – why are you leading?

**Authority** – people respond to your lead

**Strategy –** know where you are going

**Compassion –** do they know you care?

*(excerpt from* **'Legacy of Leadership'** *by Bob 'Idea Man' Hooey available from www.SuccessPublications.ca)*

*Bob visiting the Terracotta warriors in China*

# A leadership review or check-up

Take a few minutes and reflect on these probing questions around your leadership role, responsibility, and skills. Briefly record your thoughts. Being honest in recognizing your strengths and areas of growth is one of the characteristics of the top global leaders. Asking for help or getting coaching is another.

**What is your *personal* vision for your leadership role?**

**What are your specific areas of responsibility?**
- 
- 

**What strengths and skills do you bring to the role?**
- 
- 

**What leadership areas do you need help in developing?**
- 
- 

**Where do you need to draw on the skills of your fellow leaders, employees or engage a leadership coach?**
- 
-

*"A big man (or woman) is one who makes us feel bigger when we are with them."* **John C. Maxwell**

Have you ever spent time with someone who just made you feel better about yourself? Have you ever spent time with someone who left you drained, demotivated, and in a worse mood than when you met them? Who would you choose to spend time with or want to work with in a project?

**The first, of course!** Me too!

There is a secret lesson for leaders, more so for volunteer teams, in how to release the best from your team. Make them feel better about themselves for being involved with you in the project, business or organization.

This is also valid when you are in a formal leadership role and want to see your team work better together in their efforts to reach an agreed goal or deadline.

---

*"The final test of a leader is that he leaves behind him (her) in other men and women the conviction and the will to carry on… The genius of a good leader is to leave behind a situation which common sense, without the grace of genius, can deal with successfully."* **Walter Lippmann**

Remember, the *larger* view of your role as a leader is recruiting, training, equipping, and inspiring other strong leaders. Too often, we get side-tracked in the day-to-day *stuff* of work. This is important, but it is not leadership. At best, spending time working on activities might be good management, but it is not good leadership.

Invest your time working along with people if you want to be a good leader. Coach, mentor, encourage and inspire them to grow and to succeed.

The test of a true leader is in the *legacy of leadership* and productive leaders they leave behind. Invest in those who will enhance your legacy and help them create and leave their own.

---

*"The best executive is the one who has sense enough to pick good people to do what they want done, and the self-restraint to keep from meddling with them while they do it"* **Theodore Roosevelt**

This might be your biggest leadership challenge. If you suffer from this *meddling malaise*, know that you are not alone.

Thousands of well-meaning leaders dilute and undermine their leadership power by doing this with those they hope to lead, nurture, and encourage to grow and succeed.

Part of your *larger* role as a leader is equipping those you lead to succeed. This means giving them opportunities to fail or succeed, without your *constant* hands-on supervision.

So, make sure you pick good people, give them good direction and instruction and, then, give them room to find their own *unique* way of handling it. You might learn something new and they often will amaze you.

---

*"The quality of leadership, more than any other single factor, determines the success or failure of any organization."* **Fred Diedler & Martin Chemers**

You, as the leader, hold the power of success or failure within your team, company, or organization. Your actions can **inspire** them to greater effort and long-term success.

Your well-meaning or *mis*-directed actions can also **demotivate** them and sabotage their best efforts to effectively do their jobs.

Selective, **leveraged** use of your power of influence within your organization or team might be your most important contribution on your leadership agenda.

As the leader, your actions **impact** those you lead and the end results of their efforts.

If you want your leadership to count and you want your team or organization to grow and win; remember, your personal **example** leads the way.

**Walk-your-talk** is not just lip service to success, it is a real path to upward growth and mobility in the health of your organization.

---

*"In organizations, real power is generated through relationships. The patterns of relationships and the capacities to form them are more important than task, functions, roles, and positions."* **Margaret Wheatly**

Relationships define your success as a leader. Relationships inspire, create synergy, and generate enthusiasm and excitement within an organization.

It has been said, *"People don't leave jobs – they leave managers!"* This can make or break you and your team.

*Bob speaking in Paris, France*

Relationships are the key to your on-going success or failure as a leader. **You win when your team wins!**

Investing time and energy in your key relationships is critical to you, as a leader. People might work for you because of your title, but they will walk through fire *'if'* their relationship with you is a good one.

Build relationships of trust and mutual respect and see everyone on your team grow and win.

*"The quality of a person's life is in direct proportion to their commitment to excellence, regardless of their chosen field of endeavor."*
**Vince Lombardi**

**Ever notice** how some people seem to be having more fun or enjoying the fruits of their leadership efforts? Hmmm...

**Ever notice** how some people enjoy a better quality of life regardless of their income of status in life? Hmmm...

**Ever notice** how some leaders seem to have well-functioning teams with relatively few challenges? Hmmm...

I wonder if Vince's statement provides any insight into why this happens?

What do you think?

What has been your experience in this area?

Do you find these questions ring true in your life and leadership?

If not, do you think this might be an area in which you could explore or experiment?

**I wish you well in your continued growth in your leadership journey.**

*"Good plans shape good decisions. That's why good planning helps to make elusive dreams come true."*
**Lester R. Bittel**

Leaders see the ***big picture*** (vision) and have the daunting task of translating that vision into management steps and use-it-now processes for their teams to deal with, follow, and to help them succeed. Often, a dream or goal can seem elusive and challenging.

One of the techniques of successful leaders is taking the dream (goal) and breaking it down into its essential components and then looking at the process necessary to make each work in the overall picture. This is ***strategic planning at its best*** and lays out a roadmap for your team to successfully travel.

**Good planning helps focus** your thoughts and helps those you lead see where you want to take them. Engage them and share this success planning process with them.

---

*"If I have seen farther than others, it is because I was standing on the shoulders of giants."* **Isacc Newton**

Who has helped you increase your vision? Who has helped you see the bigger picture? Who has help you see your leadership role in a larger perspective?

Leaders see and share the big picture with their teams; but first, they need to see it themselves. That means, as a leader, remaining open to learning from those who have gone before you. This means building on strong foundations for success that have been laid in advance of your leadership role.

15

It also means thinking about the leaders who will follow you. That decision means equipping them to lead and to build on the strong foundations you and your team have laid. It helps put your leadership role and your investment in others into a longer perspective.

*"There is no contest between the company that buys the grudging compliance of its work force and the company that enjoys the enterprising participation of its employees."* **Richardo Sempler**

You'd think this observation would be obvious to those in leadership? Sadly, not by the way too many companies operate today! **Time after time, companies find themselves struggling and pushing their work teams to do more with less.**

At the same time, *some* companies find their teams (who are involved) stepping up to the plate and finding creative solutions to those challenges; putting in extra effort to help the company grow and move past their competition. The reason behind this success is how they (employees) are treated by the company leaders. You, as a leader, have the opportunity to create this kind of engagement and commitment by your staff and your teams.

*"An empowered organization is one in which individuals have the knowledge, skill, desire, and opportunity to personally succeed in a way that leads to collective organizational success."*
**Stephen R. Covey**

**You win when your team wins!** should be your mantra or rallying cry as a leader. It is about them and your role in helping them succeed.

Your success is **directly** tied to how successful they are in their respective roles. Wise leaders have learned this secret of **leveraged ability** in building great teams and winning organizations.

**Are you a wise leader?**

We hear the word empowerment a lot. Sadly, its **actions** are not as evident in companies around the globe. You, as a wise leader, can pay more than lip service to this worthwhile ideal. You have the power to make it a real force in your team and work environment.

---

*"No man (or woman) will make a great leader who wants to do it all my themselves, for to get all the credit for doing it."* **Andrew Carnegie**

The concept of *effective* leadership is getting things done by the most effect use of the talents and skills of others. The **secret of effective leadership** is in helping build others into stronger leaders who themselves enhance the desired results.

The wise leader is one who shares credit liberally and ensures those who contributed to the success, share in the success and recognition. These are the leaders whose teams will *walk through fire* to help them succeed or deal with sudden changes or demands experienced along the route.

Funny how some leaders (managers) haven't learned this lesson and find their teams less responsive and less willing to go the extra mile in getting things done. **Their loss!**

*"Just because you have the skill, does not mean you have the time!"* **Bob 'Idea Man' Hooey**

Leaders often lead a hectic schedule and effective ones have learned to delegate to leverage their own results. They have learned that their role is to get things done through effective use of the talents and skills of others, not just to do things. Their time is extremely valuable, and they have learned to leverage it for best impact.

Many leaders have carved out their roles based on successful application and often hands-on activities. Many find it hard to let go and to allow those they lead to work their way through challenges and jobs that they, as leaders, know they can do better.

Your leadership role is to recruit, train, and equip others to grow into their personal leadership roles. That choice is the best investment of your time within your organization.

**Investing in the growth of your team is where each of you succeeds.**

---

*"People are always blaming their circumstances for what they are. I don't believe in circumstances. The people who get on in this world are the people who get up and look for the circumstances they want, and if they can't find them, make them."*
**George Bernard Shaw**

This is where your leadership provides the model for those who follow. This is where you get the opportunity to **walk-your-talk** and lead your team profitably to the next level of success.

People can always find an excuse for not accomplishing a goal or task. However, to the true leader, excuses are never acceptable. There are reasons and factors which impact any circumstance and they can be handled and overcome.

Challenge your team to bring their suggestions or solutions along with their challenges and you equip them to over-come them. Support them as they endeavor to grow by allowing them to see new innovative solutions to their challenges and problems.

---

*"Treat people as if they were what they ought to be and you help them become what they are capable of being."* **Johann Wolfgang Von Goethe**

This is both the most rewarding and the most frustrating part of leadership. Working with people who are imperfect as yourself. 😊 Working with people who have challenges, character flaws, and other obstacles that often stop them from being as successful as they could be.

As their leader, you have the unique opportunity to see past these areas and to see them as they could be. You also have a great opportunity to work with them to grow and to move to higher levels of performance that they, themselves, never imagined.

You, as their leader, have the pure pleasure of seeing them respond, grow and move into being more productive in their lives and their roles.

**This is the true payment for leading!**

---

> *"The task of leadership is not to put greatness into people, but to elicit it, for the greatness is already there."* **John Buchan**

Remember a time when you succeeded and one of the factors of that success was the belief expressed in you by someone you respected? Their ***expressed belief*** allowed you to dig into the skills, talents, and greatness within yourself to find the strength and wisdom to deal with the task at hand.

Our roles, as leaders, are to equip and motivate our teams to believe in their own power and success. We have the unique role of being their cheerleaders, coaches, and often champions of their success.

**Their greatness lies within!** Our role, as leaders, is to draw that greatness out and to see it shine in the light of success. Great leaders allow those who follow to access, hone, and step out to share their own greatness.

---

> *"Leadership and learning are indispensable to each other."* **John F. Kennedy**

*"For the leader, school is never out!"* This simple truth is based on the premise that leadership is a ***learn-as-you-grow*** choice.

As a leader, you work with people to accomplish specific objectives and goals. However, people can be challenging. Each is different: each has different needs, desires, dreams, skills, and failings.

Your role is to *blend individuals* into various teams and into roles that best use their strengths, allowing them to grow and you to accomplish specific goals. This can be a real learning curve itself, and about yourself in your role as leader.

The more you learn, the better you can leverage that learning or skill to reach your respective goals.

The more you learn about your team, the better you can help them grow and succeed in reaching their goals.

---

*"Outstanding leaders go out of their way to boost the self-esteem of their personnel. If people believe in themselves, it's amazing what they can accomplish."*
**Sam Walton**

You would think this would be so obvious to anyone in a leadership role that they would make it a priority.

However, too many people in leadership either have no idea how this works, or they don't care about their teams. Their end results demonstrate that lack of caring.

Do you want your team to grow, to improve, and to win? Do you want them to find increased satisfaction from their involvement and activities? Do you want to be a real coach, cheerleader and champion in their lives?

If you want to be an effective leader who leads a positive legacy, I would hope so! Each day and in each interaction with your team or staff members you have this choice.

**Choose wisely!**

---

*"Leadership is not magnetic personality, that can just as well be a glib tongue. It is not 'making friends and influencing people' that is flattery. Leadership is lifting a person's vision to higher sights, the raising of a person's performance to a higher standard, the building of a personality beyond its normal limitations."* **Peter F. Drucker**

As leaders, we have the responsibility of seeing those we lead grow and become more productive in their lives and careers. We have the distinct privilege to see them as they could be. In communicating that vision or their potential, but in also being a coach and champion, we make that enhancement and success a reality.

Over the years this result has given me the greatest sense of pleasure and achievement – seeing those I worked with find their own leadership and move up to be more successful in their own efforts and activities.

---

*"The key to successful leadership today is influence, not authority."* **Kenneth Blanchard**

The days of being ***'the boss'*** are long dead, if your desire is to be an effective, inspiring leader. People today, especially our younger team members, will not simply follow your lead because you have a title.

Want to be an effective leader and see your team win? Want to see your role be one of success for you?

Focus on being a leader of influence with those you lead. This is especially true for volunteer teams where people come for their own purposes and agendas. This is true for those whose work time with you is focused on what they want or can get from it.

Leadership skills are changing. They need to in order to effectively engage and empower your team members to do their jobs.

**You win when your team wins!** Focus your energies on leading for shared success.

---

*"Think of managing change as an adventure. It tests your skills and abilities. It brings forth talent that may have been dormant. Change is also a training ground for leadership. When we think of leaders, we remember times of change, innovation, and conflict. Leadership is often about shaping a new way of life. To do that, you must advance change, take risks and accept responsibility for making change happen."*
**Charles E. Rice**

There is a major difference between being a *leader* and being a *manager.* Both have their place, but only *one* moves the organization ahead to the next level of challenge or shared success.

When things are moving ahead smoothly, being a manager can work fine. However, when your team runs into a challenge, then the leader must step up to 'lead' them through it and to greater success.

**Are you a leader or a manager?** We need more leaders and I hope you step up to that role.

---

*"The leaders who work most effectively, it seems to me, never say "I." And that is not because they have trained themselves not to say "I." They don't think "I." They think "WE." They think "Team!" They understand their job is to make the team function. They accept responsibility and don't sidestep it, but "WE" gets the credit... this is what creates trust, what enables you to get the task done."*
**Peter Drucker**

Effective leadership is about shared or team success. It is not about you and your personal or positional success.

**You win when your team wins!** This means your focus needs to remain on training, equipping, and motivating them to rise to the challenge and to grow and to succeed in their respective roles. This means **you become their coach, cheerleader, and champion in the process.**

Being an effective leader means focusing on their success because you realize that will help ensure your own.

---

*"Leadership is understanding people and involving them to help you do a job. That takes all of the characteristics, like integrity, dedication of purpose, selflessness, knowledge, skill, implacability, as well as determination not to accept a failure."*
**Admiral Arleigh A. Burke**

Leadership is about working effectively and strategically with people. It is about helping them grow and succeed. It is about leveraging and honing their skills, dreams, desires, experience, and expertise to get the job done.

Effective leaders *deliberately* invest their time with their team members to make sure they understand how to best use their respective skills and to make sure they (team) know what needs to be done to succeed.

**Leadership is a 'commitment', not a label!** That commitment takes time and effort. When you invest in your team you invest in those who hold your future success.

---

*"As we, the leaders deal with tomorrow, our task is not to try to make perfect plans. Our task is to create organizations that are sufficiently flexible and versatile that they can take our own imperfect plans and make them work in execution. That is the essential character of the learning organization."*
**Gordon R. Sullivan & Michael V. Harper**

Leadership is a learn-as-you-grow skill. Be nice if you could just read a few books (like this one) and become an amazing leader, wouldn't it? 😊

We have the ongoing challenge of working with people who are often learning as they grow. That makes leadership a bit more challenging, but it is also more rewarding when we see them succeed.

Build flexibility into your plans and agenda to ensure you are able to deal with the detours, road-blocks, and pot-holes along the way. Both you and your team will have an easier ride when you do.

**Plans are meant to be adapted and tweaked** as we go, so allow them to be.

---

> *"The task of the leader is to get his people from where they are to where they have not been."*
> **Henry Kissinger**

The leader has the challenge of taking a group of independent individuals and forming them into a team or similar structure to accomplish a specific goal. **Not always so easy.**

Along the way, the leader provided the vision of where the team needs to go and has the challenge of ensuring they effectively communicate that vision clearly to their respective teams. Again, not always so easy in today's hectic world.

As a leader, it is imperative that you are clear on your vision and goal and that you invest the time to ensure you have clearly communicated it. If not, your team will struggle and flounder until you do so.

Remember, if it was easy, everyone would be doing it, and they wouldn't need you in their lives. It isn't, and you have chosen this challenging yet important path of leadership.

---

> *"The quality of a leader is reflected in the standards they set for themselves."* **Ray Kroc**

This has become *painfully* obvious in companies and teams around the world. We see companies going down and learn about the actions of their leaders who caused the failures.

Watch the staff or team members in action and you frequently see the values as defined by the actions of their leaders. Just like *our kids*, our teams model what we do, not what we say. If we are diligent, focused, and come to work ready to work, on time – often they will too.

But, when you model the reverse, don't be surprised when they slack off and it becomes noticeable on the job or in the task.

You are their *role model* in demonstrating values, integrity, honesty, and how you deal with and value people. They will take that model into consideration of their interaction with your customers.

A valuable or costly lesson depending how you walk your talk.

---

*"Never hire or promote in your own image. It is foolish to replicate your strength and idiotic to replicate your weakness. It is essential to employee, trust, and reward those whose perspective, ability, and judgement are radically different from yours. It is also rare, for it requires uncommon humility, tolerance, and wisdom."* **Dee W. Hock**

The *wise* leader hires to compliment their strengths; to add to their wisdom and skills needed to complete the goal.

The *wise* leader hires people who can do the job and can often do it better than the leader.

The *wise* leader hires and promotes based on abilities and skills to do the job and not just because they like or relate to any particular person.

Often, the team is strengthened when the leader has the courage to surround themselves with those who see it differently and yet want to see it succeed. **Choose wisely!**

---

*"The most dangerous leadership myth is that leaders are born – that there is a genetic factor to leadership. This myth asserts that people either have certain charismatic qualities or not. That's nonsense; in fact, the opposite is true. Leaders are made rather than born."*
**Warren G. Bennis**

True, there are some people who seem to seek out leadership roles; but most leaders grew into their respective roles one commitment, one leadership activity at a time.

Each of us has *within us* the desire to take personal leadership over our lives, choices, and activities. This is the foundation for strong leadership as you must have personal leadership and responsibility before you can succeed in more formal or positional leadership roles.

Leadership is a choice, a commitment to serve, **not** a label or a birthright. Leaders choose to invest themselves in the service of those they lead.

**Recently, Toastmasters International rebranded as: Where Leaders Are Made!** Our experience has taught us that people come to Toastmasters to hone their ability to speak in public. Along the way, they also learn how to become more effective leaders as they take on roles within their clubs and districts.

*"The mediocre teacher tells. The good teacher explains. The superior teacher demonstrates. The great teacher (leader) inspires."* **William A. Ward**

Did he just say teacher? How does that relate to me in my leadership role, you might ask?

Very simple. If you seek to be a **great** leader, you seek to inspire. As a leader, part of your role is that of a teacher, instructor, or coach in defining goals, honing skills, giving direction, and helping equip your team to grow and succeed.

If you want to be a **mediocre** leader 'you' *simply* tell them what to do and how to do it. They will *simply* (hopefully) follow your instructions and you get the job done. If so, you have missed a great teaching opportunity to demonstrate or inspire, so the next time they know how to do it themselves. And do it!

As a leader, the larger part of your role is creating other strong leaders. This entails being in a teaching or coaching mindset along the way. **Keep teaching – keep inspiring!**

---

*"If your actions inspire others to dream more, learn more, do more and become more, you are a leader."* **John Quincy Adams**

This, is the exciting part of leadership! This is where your actions actually **impact** those who follow and **inspire** them to be even more diligent in pursuing their dreams and growing to the next level.

**Leadership can be a lonely and challenging role.**

As a leader, there will be times when you can be overwhelmed by the activities and tough decisions you are forced to handle. Times when you are stretched.

Deal with those times and challenges; but keep your focus on being that *inspirational* leader whose life and actions set the standards and encourage those who follow to meet or exceed them. Wow!

Be that *inspirational* leader whose words and actions motivate your team to *rise-up* to tackle the big challenges, the big dreams, grow to the next level and succeed in their lives and their respective roles and duties.

Please accept my encouragement and appreciation for your leadership efforts. The world needs your leadership.

# Copyright and license notes

'Pocket Wisdom for Leaders! (Updated 4th edition)
*The Power of One!*

Bob 'Idea Man' Hooey, Accredited Speaker, 2011 Spirit of CAPS recipient. Prolific author of 30 plus business, leadership, and career success publications

© Copyright 1999-2019 Bob 'Idea Man' Hooey

**All rights reserved worldwide** *No part of this publication may be retained, copied, sold, rented or loaned, transmitted, reproduced, broadcast, performed or distributed in any such medium, or by any means, nor stored in any computer or distributed over any network without permission in writing from the publisher and/or author. Care has been taken to trace ownership of copyright material contained in this volume. Graphics are royalty free or under license. The publisher will gladly receive information that will allow him to rectify any reference or credit line in subsequent editions. Segments of this publication were originally published as articles and/or parts of other books and program materials and are included here by permission of the publishers and authors.* Unattributed quotations are by Bob 'Idea Man' Hooey.

Photos of Bob: **Dov Friedman**, www.photographybyDov.com
**Trevor Schneider**, www.interiorphotos.ca
**Bonnie-Jean McAllister**, www.elantraphotography.com
**Frédéric Bélot**, www.fredericbelot.fr/fr
Editorial, layout and design: **Irene Gaudet,** Vitrak Creative Services (a division of Creativity Corner Inc.), vitrakcreative.com

**ISBN 13: 9781798152881**

Printed in the United States 10 9 8 7 6 5 4 3 2 1
**Success Publications** – a division of Creativity Corner Inc.
Box 10, Egremont, AB T0A 0Z0
www.successpublications.ca
Creative office: 1-780-736-0009

# Acknowledgements, credits, and disclaimers

As with each of my books, a very special dedication of this piece of myself, to the two people who meant the most to me, my folks **Ron and Marge Hooey**. Sadly, both my parents left this earthly realm in 1999. I still miss our time together and your encouragement and love. I was blessed with the two of you in my life. I've added **George and Lillian Sidor** (Irene's folks) to this gratitude list.

To my inspiring wife and professional proof reader and publications coach, **Irene Gaudet**, who loves, encourages, and supports me in my quest to continue sharing my **Ideas At Work!** across the world. Thank you seems so inadequate for your timely work in helping make my writing and my client service better! I love the time we spend together!

To my colleagues and friends in the National Speakers Association (NSA), the Canadian Association of Professional Speakers (CAPS), and the Global Speakers Federation (GSF) who continually challenge me to strive for success and increased excellence.

To my great audiences, leaders, students, coaching clients, and readers across the globe who share their experiences and enjoyment of my work. Your positive and supportive feedback encourages me to keep working on additional programs and success publications like this updated version. My experience with you creates the foundation for additional real-life experiences I can take from the stage to the page, the classroom to the boardroom.

My thanks to a select few friends for your ongoing support and 'constructive' abuse. You know who you are. ☺

# Disclaimer

*We have not attempted to cite all the authorities and sources consulted in the preparation of this book. To do so would require much more space than is available. The list would include departments of various governments, libraries, industrial institutions, periodicals, and many individuals. Inspiration was drawn from many sources, including other books by the author; in this updated creation of* **Pocket Wisdom for Leaders.**

*This book is written and designed to provide information on more effective use of your time, as a life and leadership enhancement guide. It is sold with the 'explicit' understanding that the publisher and/or the author are not engaged in rendering legal, accounting, or other Professional services. If legal or other expert assistance is required, the services of a competent Professional in your geographic area should be sought.*

*It is not the purpose of this book to reprint all the information that is otherwise available. Its primary purpose is to complement, amplify, and supplement other books and reference materials already available. You are encouraged to search out and study all the available material, learn as much as possible, and tailor the information to your individual needs. This will help to enhance your success in being a more effective sales person, leader or professional.*

*Every effort has been made to make this book as complete and as accurate as possible within the scope of its focus. However, there may be mistakes, both typographical and in content or attribution. Graphics are royalty free or under license. Care has been taken to trace ownership of copyright material contained in this volume. The publisher will gladly receive information that will allow him to rectify any reference or credit line in subsequent editions. This book should be used only as a general guide and not as the ultimate source of information. Furthermore, this book contains information that is current only up to the date of publication.*

*The purpose of* **Pocket Wisdom for Leaders** *is to educate and entertain; perhaps to inform and to inspire. It is certainly to challenge its readers to learn and apply its secrets and tips, to challenge them to enhance their skills and leverage their time to create more Productive outcomes. The author and publisher shall have neither liability nor responsibility to any person or entity with respect to any loss or damage caused, or alleged to have been caused, directly or indirectly, by the information contained in this book.*

# Bob's B.E.S.T. publications

Bob is a prolific author who has been capturing and sharing his wisdom and experience in print and electronic formats for the past fifteen plus years. In addition to the following publications, several of them best sellers, he has written for consumer, corporate, professional associations, trade, and on-line publications. He has been engaged to write and assist on publications by other best-selling writers and  successful companies. Some of his publications are listed below.

Bob's **B**usiness **E**nhancement **S**uccess **T**ools

**Leadership, business, and career success series**

**Running TOO Fast** (8th edition 2018)
**Legacy of Leadership** (3rd edition 2016)
**Make ME Feel Special!** (6th edition 2016)
**Why Didn't I 'THINK' of That?** (5th edition 2015)
**Speaking for Success!** (8th edition 2016)
**THINK Beyond the First Sale** (3rd edition 2017)
**Prepare Yourself to WIN!** (3rd edition 2018)

**Bob's mini-book success series**

**The Courage to Lead!** (4th edition 2017)
**Creative Conflict** (3rd edition 2017)

**Get to YES!** (3rd edition 2017)
**THINK Before You Ink!** (3rd edition 2017)
**Running to Win!** (2nd edition 2017)
**How to Generate More Sales** (4th edition 2017)
**Unleash your Business Potential** (3rd edition 2017)
**Learn to Listen** (2nd edition 2017)
**Creativity Counts!** (3rd edition 2016)
**Create Your Future!** (3rd edition 2017)

**Co-authored books created by Bob**

Quantum Success – 3 volume series (2006)
In the Company of Leaders (3rd edition 2014)
Foundational Success (2nd edition 2013)

**Bob's Pocket Wisdom series:** *(coming as e-books in 2019)*

Pocket Wisdom for **Selling Professionals** (updated 2019)
Pocket Wisdom for **Speakers** (updated 2019)
Pocket Wisdom for **Innovators**
Pocket Wisdom for **Leaders – Power of One!** (updated 2019)
Pocket Wisdom for **Business Builders**

**Bob's Idea-rich leaders edge series:** *(new 2018-2019)*

**LEAD!** 12 idea-rich leadership success strategies
**CREATE!** Idea-rich strategies for enhanced innovation
**TIME!** Idea-rich tips for enhanced performance and productivity
**SERVE!** Idea-rich strategies for enhanced customer service
**SPEAK!** Idea-rich tips and techniques for great presentations
**CREATIVE CONFLICT** Idea-rich leadership for team success
**SELL!** Idea-rich techniques for sales success

**Visit: www.SuccessPublications.ca** for more information on Bob's publications and other success resources. Email bob@successpublications.ca

# What they say about Bob 'Idea Man' Hooey

As I travel across North America, and around the globe, sharing my **Ideas At Work!** I am fortunate to get feedback and comments from my audiences and colleagues. These comments come from people who have been touched, challenged, or simply enjoyed themselves in one of my sessions. **I'd love to come and share some ideas with your organization and teams.**

*"I still get comments from people about your presentation. Only a few speakers have left an impression that lasts that long. You hit a spot with the tourism people."* **Janet Bell**, Yukon Economic Forums

*"Thank you, Bob, it is always a pleasure to see a true professional at work. You have made the name 'Speaker' stand out as a truism - someone who encourages people to examine their lives and adjust. The personal stories you shared with your audience made such a great impression on everyone. The comments indicated you hit people right where it is important - in their hearts. Each of those in your audience took away a new feeling of personal success and encouragement."* **Sherry Knight**, Dimension Eleven Human Resources and Communications

*"I am pleased to recommend Bob 'Idea Man' Hooey to any organization looking for a charismatic, confident speaker and seminar leader. I have seen Bob in action on several occasions, and he is ALWAYS on! Bob has the ability to grab his audience's attention and keep it. Quite simply, if Bob is involved - your program or seminar is guaranteed to succeed."* **Maurice Laving**, Coordinator Training and Development, London Drugs

*"On very short notice Bob cleared his schedule and graciously presented at our meeting when the original Speaker was unable to attend. **Last week Bob set the tone for our two-day leadership meeting and gave us all a motivational lift.** His compassion and true interest in people was clearly evident, making him very credible. He shared some great stories, has a wealth of experience and knowledge and it was a pleasure listening to him. His down-to-Earth style makes it easier to retain the information presented. He also followed up with additional info and handouts, cementing his message of building bridges, not walls. Fantastic job, Bob, and thanks again!"* **Barbara Afra Beler**, MBA, Senior Specialist Commercial Community, Alberta North, **BMO Bank of Montreal**

*"I have been so excited working with Bob Hooey, as he has given inspiration and motivation to our leadership team members. Both at the Brick Warehouse – Alberta and here at Art Van Furniture – Michigan; with his years of experience in working with business executives and his humorous and delightful packaging of his material, he makes learning with Bob a real joy. But most importantly, anyone who encounters his material is the better for it."* **Kim Yost**, former CEO Art Van Furniture, former CEO The Brick

**Motivate your teams**, your employees, and your leaders to 'productively' grow and 'profitably' succeed!

**Protect your conference investment** - leverage your training dollars.

**Enhance your professional career** and sell more products and services.

**Equip and motivate your leaders** and their teams to grow and succeed, 'even' in tough times!

**Leverage your time** to enhance your skills, equip your teams, and better serve your clients.

**Leverage your leadership** and investment of time to leave a significant legacy!

**Call today** to engage best-selling author, award winning, inspirational leadership keynote speaker, leaders' success coach, and employee development trainer**, Bob 'Idea Man' Hooey** and his innovative, audience based, results-focused, **Ideas At Work!** for your next company, convention, leadership, staff, training, or association event. You'll be glad you did!

**Call 1-780-736-0009** to connect with Bob 'Idea Man' Hooey today! Visit: www.ideaman.net or www.BobHooey.training for more information.

# Thanks for reading *Pocket Wisdom for Leaders*

Each time I prepare to step on the stage; each time I sit down to write, or in this case to update and re-write, I am challenged to ensure I deliver something that will be of **use-it-now value** to my reader.

- I ask myself, "If I was reading this, what would I be looking for?"
- As well as, "Why is this relevant to me, today?"

**These two questions help to keep me focused** and help me to remain clear on my objectives. They help to remind me to dig into my experiences, stories, examples, and research to provide solid information that will be of benefit and help my readers, when they apply it, succeed. That can be an exciting challenge!

I trust I have done that for you in this updated primer. **Pocket Wisdom for Leaders** is my attempt to capture some of the lessons learned *first-hand* serving on various teams and in leadership roles and to share them with you. We need more leaders, now, more than ever. The world is crying out for more compassionate and courageous leaders. I hope you will step up and step into your role as a more effective and influential leader.

*Bob in Mumbai, India*

I'd love to hear from you and read your success stories. If you would be so kind, please drop me a quick email at: **bob@ideaman.net**

**Bob 'Idea Man' Hooey**
**2011 Spirit of CAPS recipient**
www.ideaman.net
www.BobHooey.training

www.ingramcontent.com/pod-product-compliance
Lightning Source LLC
Chambersburg PA
CBHW071158220526
45468CB00003B/1064